HJ

D0783780

For Rosalie, Aimé and Barnabé
V. A.

For Alain and Jérôme, the bird fisherman
E. T.

To explain my love of birds.
I have very often been asked to justify this love.
What is there to say? I love them, that is all there is to it.

Paul Ardenne,
Art historian and author of
Comment je suis oiseau, Le Passage publications

Franklin Watts
First published in Great Britain in 2016 by The Watts Publishing Group

Original title: INVENTAIRE ILLUSTRÉ DES OISEAUX
© 2015 Albin Michel Jeunesse
Copyright English translation © The Watts Publishing Group, 2016

We would like to thank Jean-Philippe Siblet, a trained ornithologist and Director of the Department of Natural Heritage at the National Museum of Natural History, France.

Credits
Photoengraving: IGS-CP (16)
Graphics and production: cedricramadier.com
Translation: PS Translations
Editorial for this edition: Rachel Cooke
Design for this edition: Peter Scoulding

ISBN 978 1 4451 5131 1

Printed in China.

Franklin Watts
An imprint of
Hachette Children's Group
Part of The Watts Publishing Group
Carmelite House
50 Victoria Embankment
London EC4Y 0DZ

An Hachette UK Company
www.hachette.co.uk

www.franklinwatts.co.uk

Illustrated
COMPENDIUM
of BIRDS

Virginie
Aladjidi

Emmanuelle
Tchoukriel

W
FRANKLIN WATTS
LONDON•SYDNEY

INTRODUCTION

Welcome to this *Illustrated Compendium of Birds*. What are birds? They are animals that fly, lay eggs and have a beak, but so do other animals – the bat flies and it is a mammal; the snail (a gastropod) and fish lay eggs; the turtle (a reptile) or the octopus (a cephalopod) also have a beak … What makes birds unique and enables scientists to put them in a separate class from all other animals is **their feathers, thousands of which cover their bodies and their wings.**

Birdsong in the garden, a call in the woods, a silhouette in the sky, a nest up on the roof, a feather found on the ground … each one is a clue to spot birds, to recognise them and name them. There are about 10,000 species of bird worldwide; this *Illustrated Compendium* features nearly 80 of them and gives lots of information about how to identify them. Each bird's plumage is described and, where relevant, its song. We give the bird's size and, in most cases, its wingspan. If a bird is not found in Britain, we state where it lives. In addition a surprising fact about the species is given, for example about its food or how it attracts a mate. The birds are grouped by their order – the name that scientists use to separate birds into types in a process called classification.

Emmanuelle Tchoukriel, a scientific illustrator, creates her subtle images of birds with great poetry. Her Indian ink and watercolours bring them to life, just like the natural history illustrators who drew birds before photography and film took over.

In recognition of these earlier illustrators, Emmanuelle has called her pictures "plates", referring to the method of printing books then that used engraved stone or metal plates.

We hope this book will inspire and amaze readers about the extraordinary world of birds. Watch and listen carefully … What birds can you spot?

Virginie Aladjidi

CONTENTS

Small illustrated bird dictionary —————————————————————————— pages 8 to 10

Part One: THE PASSERIFORMES ———————————————————————— plates 1 to 23

Part Two: OTHER BIRDS ———————————————————————————— plates 24 to 59

The cuculiformes, such as the common cuckoo ———————————— plates 24 to 25

The coraciiformes, such as the hoopoe ————————————————— plates 26 to 27

The piciformes, such as the great spotted woodpecker ——————— plates 28 to 29

The strigiformes, such as the barn owl ————————————————— plates 30 to 31

The apodiformes, such as the hummingbirds ——————————————— plates 32 to 33

The galliformes, such as the Reeves' pheasant ————————————— plates 34 to 35

The psittaciformes, such as the scarlet macaw ——————————————— plates 36 to 39

The pelecaniformes, such as the scarlet ibis ——————————————— plates 40 to 43

The ciconiiformes, such as storks ———————————————————— plates 44 to 45

The anseriformes, such as the greylag goose ———————————————— plate 46

The falconiformes, such as the golden eagle ——————————————— plates 47 to 48

The charadriiformes, such as the black-headed gull ————————— plates 49 to 53

The procellariiformes, such as the wandering albatross ——————————— plate 54

The sphenisciformes, such as the emperor penguin ——————————————— plate 55

The struthioniformes, such as the ostrich ——————————————— plates 56 to 57

The gruiformes, such as the black-crowned crane ——————————————— plate 58

The phoenicopteriformes, such as the greater flamingo ——————————— plate 59

Glossary —————————————————————————————————————— page 76

Index of plates ———————————————————————————————— page 78

SMALL ILLUSTRATED BIRD DICTIONARY

Identifying birds

To identify a bird, we can describe its shape, and above all the colours of the plumage on its body, on its wings, its tail, its head or that of its beak and its legs.

The bird's head

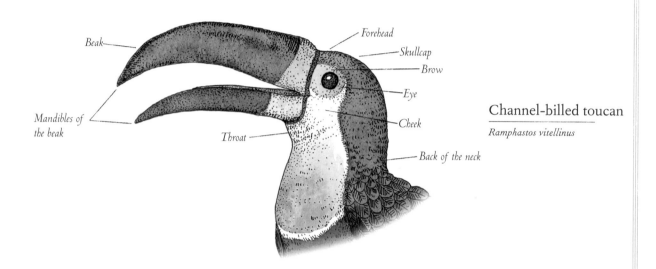

Beak

Forehead
Skullcap
Brow

Eye

Mandibles of
the beak

Throat

Cheek

Back of the neck

Channel-billed toucan

Ramphastos vitellinus

General silhouette

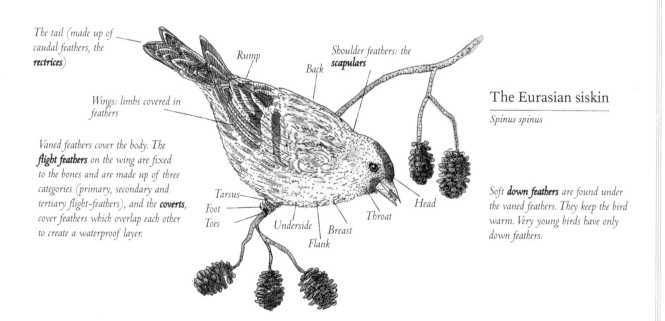

The tail (made up of
caudal feathers, the
rectrices)

Rump

Shoulder feathers: the
scapulars

Back

Wings: limbs covered in
feathers

Vaned feathers cover the body. The
flight feathers on the wing are fixed
to the bones and are made up of three
categories (primary, secondary and
tertiary flight-feathers), and the **coverts**,
cover feathers which overlap each other
to create a waterproof layer.

Tarsus
Foot
Toes

Underside

Breast
Flank

Head

Throat

The Eurasian siskin

Spinus spinus

Soft **down feathers** are found under
the vaned feathers. They keep the bird
warm. Very young birds have only
down feathers.

Birds' bones are light and sometimes hollow. Their powerful lungs and heart help them extract the energy from their food, which is needed for flight in the majority of birds. The size of the heart may increase slightly in migratory birds, so that they can fly long distances.

The feathers

Birds moult regularly with new feathers replacing the old ones, which wears out with use. The frequency of the moult varies from bird to bird: some moult three times a year, while others will only renew their plumage every three years.

The plumage of certain species is highly coloured during the mating season (usually in the spring), then replaced by duller coloured feathers for the winter. This is the case in some types of duck, for example. The plumage of the males is generally more colourful than that of the females, as the latter must be camouflaged when they hatch their eggs and care for their young.

A primary flight feather

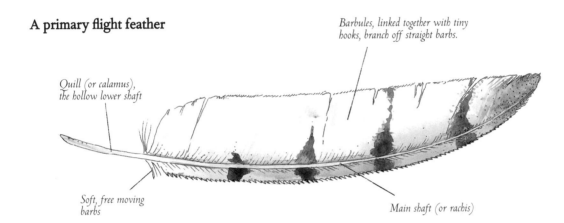

Barbules, linked together with tiny hooks, branch off straight barbs.

Quill (or calamus), the hollow lower shaft

Soft, free moving barbs

Main shaft (or rachis)

A down feather

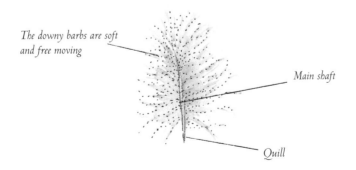

The downy barbs are soft and free moving

Main shaft

Quill

The adult swan is the bird with the most feathers: it may have as many as 25,000!

Birds most commonly flap their wings to fly around:

The bird regularly flaps its wings, sometimes interrupting this in order to glide (like the pigeon seen here). The tail wings are usually closed, but spread to land or attract a mate.

Depending on the species, the bird also uses:

Soaring: the bird lets itself be taken up by warm air currents, in a circular pattern. At high altitude it glides, like the buzzard (see plate 47).

Gliding flight: the bird slides through the air without flapping its wings, gaining lift from their shape. This type of flight is used a lot by large migratory birds, such as storks (see plate 44).

Hovering: the bird flaps its wings to stay in one spot, as the kestrel (see plate 48) does to locate its prey, or to gather food, such as hummingbirds (see plate 32).

Diving flight: the bird folds its wings to plunge down, like the peregrine falcon (see plate 48) or the kingfisher (above).

 *Part One*

THE PASSERIFORMES

In classification, scientists put birds into one class, such as birds, then they separate them further into orders. There are over 6,000 birds in the passeriformes order. This represents more than **60 per cent of the world's birds**. These are commonly known as "perching birds" because of the structure of four toes – three point forward and one back, allowing them to perch.

These birds have always been known for their singing and another common name for them is "songbird". Indeed, songbirds have a unique syrinx (an organ at the back of the windpipe which enables them to communicate) that is more developed than in other birds. In the syrinx, cartilage makes a membrane vibrate in front of two cavities in the throat to create the song.

Here we have illustrated 27 species of songbird: for most of them we have described their song and one of their cries. Most songbirds use song to mark their territory. The cry is more often used to express fear or to keep in contact with other birds.

Thrush

Blue tit

Cyanistes caeruleus

Average size (tail included): 11.5 cm
Average wingspan: 13 cm

The blue tit's skullcap, wings, tail, legs and toes are blue. The side of the head is white with a blue line that runs from the beak, over the eye and up to the nape of the neck. It has a yellow underside. This plump songbird is found throughout Europe, North Africa and Asia. The blue tit looks for food in trees and garden plants. It nests in the hollow of a tree and also likes nesting places put up by humans, even letterboxes – which can be a surprise for the postman! Its nest is made of moss, with final touches of wool.

🕊 The blue tit's song is clear and quite high-pitched: *"tsee-tsee-tsu-hu-hu-hu-hu"*.

— *plate 1* —

Great tit

Parus major

Average size (tail included): 14 cm
Average wingspan: 25 cm

This bird is a common visitor to our gardens. It has a black head, white cheeks, green back and stocky wings crossed in black, and a yellow breast and underside. Its varied song and metallic sounding cries can be heard throughout Europe. The great tit is very active: it looks for cracks in trees and walls for nesting, and looks for food on the ground or in tree trunks. It likes a mixed diet of insects, spiders, fruit and seeds.

🐦 The great tit produces a distinctive two-syllable song: *"teeteew teeteew" "seeseesee seeseesee"*.

Songbirds' offspring are not well developed initially, and are fed for a long time by their parents in the nest. They open their beaks to be fed.

The great tit likes to feed its young on caterpillars and may return to the nest 40 times in an hour with food.

— *plate 2* —

Robin

Erithacus rubecula

Average size (tail included): 14 cm
Average wingspan: 21 cm

This pot-bellied, restless bird is easy to recognise from its red-orange breast and its tail. The robin has a brown back, a white belly and big shiny dark eyes. A loner, it jumps along the ground, pecking at worms and insects. It guards its territory, often an area of park or garden. It is not shy and may settle next to you if you stay still.

🖝 The robin sings a series of cascading notes:
"twiddle-oo, twiddle-eedee, twiddle-oo twiddle".

Songbirds generally have two moults per year. Their old, worn out feathers fall out and their plumage is gradually renewed. This is a flight-feather from a robin.

— *plate 3* —

House sparrows

Passer domesticus

Average size (tail included): 18 cm
Average wingspan: 25 cm

This bird, which flies fast and hops along the ground, lives all over the world close to human homes (hence its name). The male has a grey breast and underside, and brown wings. During the mating season, it has a black mark on its throat, known as a "bib", which is its breeding plumage. The female's feathers are more grey. House sparrows do not migrate, but live in groups, particularly in autumn and winter.

🐦 The sparrow tweets: *"tcheep-tcheep"*.

— *plate 4* —

Goldfinch

Carduelis carduelis

Average size (tail included): 12 cm
Average wingspan: 23 cm

With its attractive red-orange head above its brown back, black, white and yellow wings, the goldfinch is fidgety and its flight is undulating. Like all finches, its beak is great for eating seeds, its main diet for a large part of the year. However it also eats insects when it is raising its young.

🦅 The elegant goldfinch trills and twitters: *"tiglit-tiglit"*.

The passeriformes take great care when building their nests. The female goldfinch lays four to six pale blue eggs with purple, red or pink spots concentrated at the larger end. Its nest is made from roots, spiders' webs and dandelion seeds, and is truly a work of art. This goldfinch nest is in a lime tree.

— *plate 5* —

Western yellow wagtail

Motacilla flava

Average size (tail included): 16 cm
Average wingspan: 27 cm

With its olive green back and a bright yellow underside, the male yellow wagtail is prepared to do all he can to attract the female. This slender bird with a long, wagging tail, breaks into song when perched on a grass stalk or a flower! During the mating season, the wagtail ruffles its breast feathers while it sings. It eats insects, which it tends to find near fields of cattle. This species is a long distance migrator that spends each winter in the southern Sahara.

The western yellow wagtail sings:
"tsweep-tsweep-tsweep".

— *plate 6* —

Common raven

Corvus corax

Average size (tail included): 64 cm
Average wingspan: 150 cm

The common raven is the largest of the passeriformes. This cautious bird has a black plumage with a hint of blue, and lives mainly in mountainous regions. Its beak is solid and its feathers are bristly around the throat. In flight, its tail forms a diamond shape. It has several very loud calls and imitates other birds, but its harsh cry is easily recognisable. Male and female stay together for life and remain in one place. Young ravens are known to be playful.

🐦 The common raven caws: *"rrok-rrok"* and *"arrk-arrk-arrk"*.

— plate 7 —

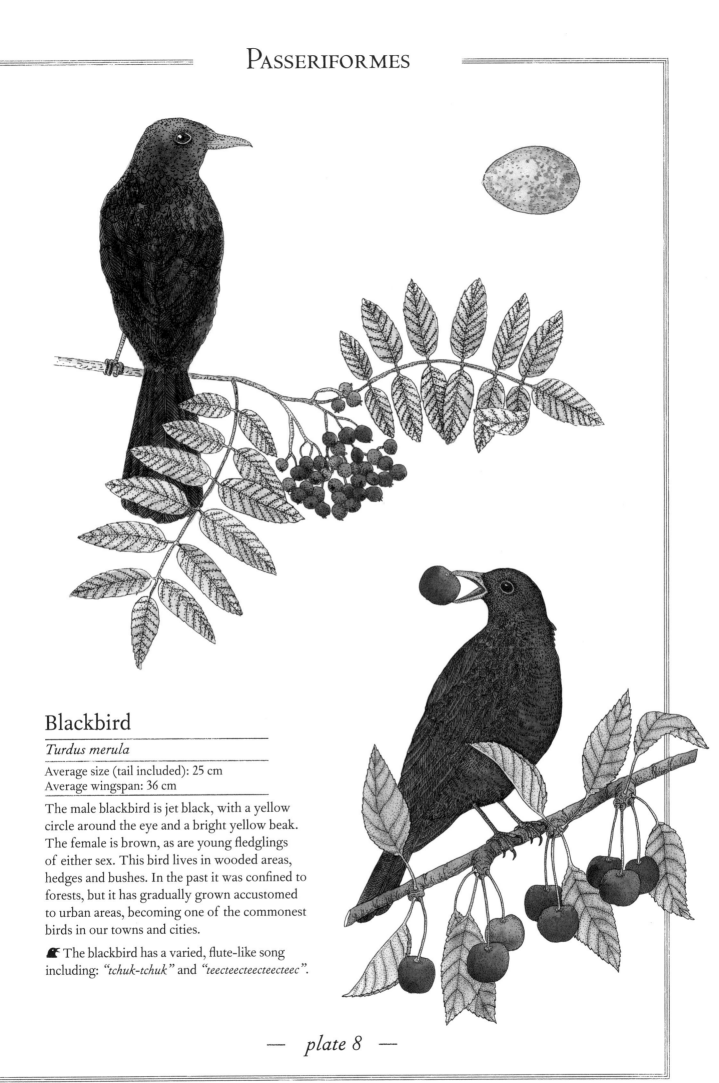

Blackbird

Turdus merula

Average size (tail included): 25 cm
Average wingspan: 36 cm

The male blackbird is jet black, with a yellow circle around the eye and a bright yellow beak. The female is brown, as are young fledglings of either sex. This bird lives in wooded areas, hedges and bushes. In the past it was confined to forests, but it has gradually grown accustomed to urban areas, becoming one of the commonest birds in our towns and cities.

The blackbird has a varied, flute-like song including: *"tchuk-tchuk"* and *"teecteecteecteecteec"*.

— *plate 8* —

Cirl bunting

Emberiza cirlus

Average size (tail included): 16 cm
Average wingspan: 23 cm

The cirl bunting's head is distinctive. It has black and yellow stripes, a green skullcap and a black bib. Its rump is grey-brown with ginger-coloured tail feathers. Its underside is yellow and its tail is elongated. Sometimes mistaken for a yellowhammer, the cirl bunting is now found only in Devon in Britain. It is more common in Southern Europe and Africa.

🐦 Cirl buntings have a rattled trill that speeds up: *"ʒeeeeet-ʒeeeeet"*.

Four or five bluish eggs, with black markings and brown strands, may be seen in the cirl bunting's nest, which it builds low down in a bush, near the ground.

— plate 9 —

Common whitethroat

Sylvia communis

Average size (tail included): 14 cm
Average wingspan: 22 cm

The common whitethroat migrates to Britain from Africa. It is difficult to spot, as it often hides in bushes, but it perches on exposed branches to sing. The male has a grey head, the female, a brown head. Both have a white throat and red-brown wings.

🐦 The common whitethroat hums and lets out a cry: *"houet-houet-houet"*.

— *plate 10* —

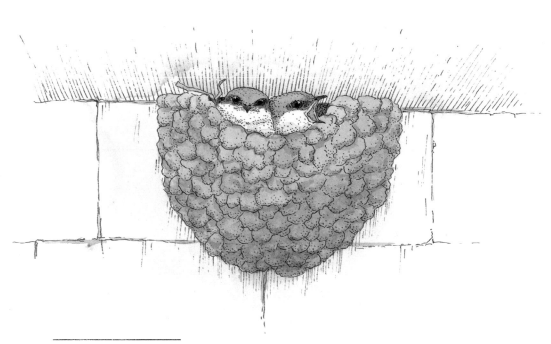

House martins collect small balls of wet mud from puddles and ponds and use them to build a mud nest. This one is globe-shaped, with a small side opening. House martins like to nest underneath the eaves of a house or a building.

House martin

Delichon urbicum

Average size (tail included): 13 cm
Average wingspan: 27 cm

The house martin can be recognised by the white area near its tail and by its pure white underside. Its tail is short and forked. Its cry is less varied than that of the swallow but still changes according to its mood and what it is doing. In winter it migrates to Africa.

🦅 The house martin emits high-pitched and liquid sounds: *"chirp-chirrip"* and *"prri"*.

— plate 11 —

Swallow,
or barn swallow

Hirundo rustica

Average size (tail included): 20 cm
Average wingspan: 33 cm

This bird has a dark red throat that can appear black from a distance, and a cream underside. Its silhouette is slender, its tail tapered. The two lateral tail feathers, also known as "streamers", are longer in the male and grow as the bird ages. The swallow moves acrobatically through the sky in order to catch its prey of flying insects. Swallows build nests from mud and bits of plants in outbuildings or roof spaces. If they can, they will repair an existing nest and use it year after year.

🦅 The swallow warbles and tweets: *"witt-witt"* or, as a warning, *"siflitt"*, a bit like the screech of an old gate!

— *plate 12* —

Bohemian waxwing

Bombycilla garrulus

Average size (tail included): 18 cm
Average wingspan: 34 cm

The waxwing has highly distinctive plumage and a
salmon pink crest. It has a black brow that extends out,
and the bottom of its back and its rump are grey. Marks
on its wings sometimes give an indication of its age.
Its short black tail is finished with a bright yellow strip.
The waxwing is a typical bird of the northern forests
of Scandinavia, Russia and Asia, but it visits Britain in
winter. Occasionally it migrates in large numbers due
to a shortage of food in its breeding areas.

🐦 The Bohemian waxwing repeats its rolling whistle:
"siirrr siirrr".

— *plate 13* —

Superb fairywren

Malurus cyaneus

Average size (tail included): 18 cm

This small songbird, found in meadows, gardens and urban areas, lives only in Australia. During the mating season, breeding males have bright blue plumage, and a black throat and band across the eye. The females have very different plumage, ranging from light to dark brown. The males are closer in colour to the females when young or not breeding. To attract a mate, the male pulls off small yellow petals and offers them to females.

🐦 The superb fairywren's song is made up of a series of loud sounds: *"tchit-tchit-tchit"*.

— *plate 14* —

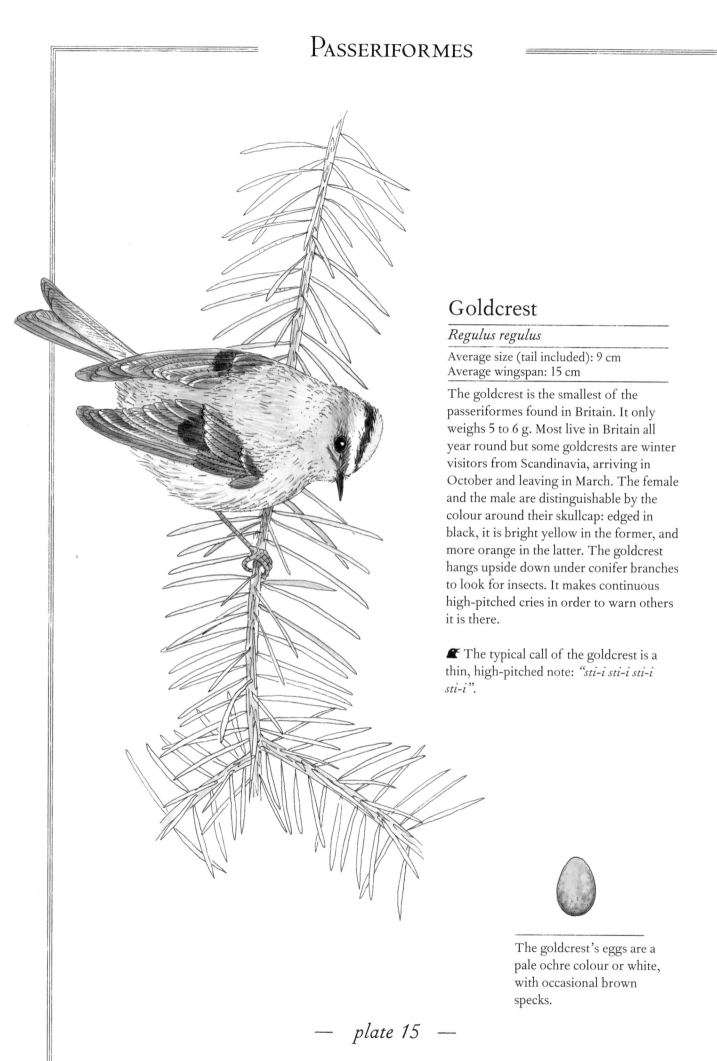

Goldcrest

Regulus regulus

Average size (tail included): 9 cm
Average wingspan: 15 cm

The goldcrest is the smallest of the passeriformes found in Britain. It only weighs 5 to 6 g. Most live in Britain all year round but some goldcrests are winter visitors from Scandinavia, arriving in October and leaving in March. The female and the male are distinguishable by the colour around their skullcap: edged in black, it is bright yellow in the former, and more orange in the latter. The goldcrest hangs upside down under conifer branches to look for insects. It makes continuous high-pitched cries in order to warn others it is there.

🐦 The typical call of the goldcrest is a thin, high-pitched note: *"sti-i sti-i sti-i sti-i"*.

The goldcrest's eggs are a pale ochre colour or white, with occasional brown specks.

— *plate 15* —

Magpie

Pica pica

Average size (tail included): 46 cm
Average wingspan: 59 cm

The magpie is a corvid, the name given to the crow family. It has a long black tail with hints of green and violet that opens into a fan. Its plumage is black on the underside of the body and on the head, and pure white on the underside and the flanks; its wings are white, edged with black. The magpie lives in a pair and is wary of humans, although it often lives in towns. It has a varied diet, including insects and food scraps, and may even raid other birds' nests for eggs or chicks. Its flight is not very steady. It is a chatty and noisy bird. Its habit of lining its nest with shiny objects, such as broken glass and metal, means that it is sometimes known as a thief, which is not in fact the case.

The magpie chatters: *"chack-chack-chack-chack"*.

The male and the female build a large nest made of branches and lined with roots. There is a sort of roof that protects the opening. On hatching, the young are fed on snails, worms, small rodents, frogs, slow worms, spiders, caterpillars, insects and grain.

— *plate 16* —

fig. 1

African stonechat

Saxicola torquata

Average size (tail included): 12 cm
Average wingspan: 20 cm

Found in Central and Southern Africa, this bird looks
very like stonechats seen in Europe. The male has
a black head, ginger throat and brown wings. The
female has no black head and her plumage is duller.
These plump songbirds live alone or in pairs in the
undergrowth, and perch on grass looking for insects.

🐦 The stonechat sings: *"ouis-trac-ouis-trac-trac"*.

Réunion stonechat,
or tec-tec

Saxicola tectes

Average size (tail included): 12.5 cm
Average wingspan: 21 cm

The Réunion stonechat is part of the stonechat
family but is a species unique to the island of
Réunion (east of Africa in the Indian Ocean). It
is very common there and often quite tame. A
solitary bird, it hunts insects in flight or on the
ground. It builds its nest on the ground, under
branches. Its eggs are a very light blue-green
colour, flecked with ginger marks. Its call is very
similar to other stonechats.

fig. 2

— plate 17 —

Chaffinch

Fringilla coelebs

Average size (tail included): 15.5 cm
Average wingspan: 26 cm

One of the most colourful birds in the finch family, the chaffinch is a common sight in Britain. Many of the population live here all year round but numbers expand with winter visitors from Northern Europe. The chaffinch favours woodland and hedgerow habitats but can be spotted just about anywhere. During the mating season, the male's plumage becomes a brighter pink on its stomach and cheeks with a grey-blue head and a brown back; his beak is grey-blue (whereas it is light brown in winter). The male starts singing in February, as if he is practising for the spring to come.

🐦 The chaffinch chirps and sings: *"pink-pink-pink"* or *"chip chip chip chooee chooee cheeoo"*.

— plate 18 —

fig. 1

Raggiana bird of paradise

Paradisaea raggiana

Average size (tail included): 33 cm
Average wingspan: 55 cm

There are around forty species of birds of paradise, famous for colourful and flamboyant plumage. The Raggiana bird of paradise lives in the rainforests of Papua New Guinea. The male has a yellow head, a green neck, a light blue beak, red wings and a pink tail during the mating season. He dances to attract a female with around twenty other males in the middle of an arena, or "lek". The female then chooses her partner.

Northern cardinal

Cardinalis cardinalis

Average size (tail included): 22 cm
Average wingspan: 28 cm

The male northern cardinal has all-crimson red plumage, like a Catholic cardinal's robes (hence its name), and has a black face mask. In the female, the mask is grey and the plumage brown-grey with touches of red. Both male and female have a strong coral-coloured beak. This bird from North America eats seeds, some insects and drinks maple sap, the sweet liquid that flows from the tree when people cut the bark open to make maple syrup from the sap.

🐦 The northern cardinal whistles clear notes: *"uit-uit"* or *"too-too"*.

fig. 2

— *plate 19* —

Crimson sunbird

Aethopyga siparaja

Average size (tail included): 11 cm

This tiny passeriforme lives in India, Indonesia and the Philippines. The male's head, the top of its back and its throat are red. Its wings are grey and its tail is dark blue. Two black lines run from its beak right to its neck. Sunbirds have metallic glints on their plumage which catch the light, giving this bird family its name. A sunbird gathers nectar from flowers using its long beak, sometime hovering like a hummingbird.

— *plate 20* —

Black redstart

Phoenicurus ochruros

Average size (tail included): 14 cm
Average wingspan: 26 cm

The male black redstart has a blacker back than the female. Its lower belly, its rump and its tail are red-orange, as its name would suggest. This bird can live up to eight years. It is rare in Britain, with a few resident and some winter visitors, but is found elsewhere in Europe, Asia and North Africa. It eats insects, fruit and tiny crustaceans that it finds on beaches.

The cries of the black redstart start with: *"tsitsitseri"* followed by a sound of crumpled paper and finish with *"tsia-tsia"*.

The eggs of European redstarts are snow-white, whereas those of the redstarts that live in Asia are blue. It is very rare to see such a difference in egg colour in birds of the same species.

— *plate 21* —

Nightingale

Luscinia megarhynchos

Average size (tail included): 16.5 cm
Average wingspan: 24 cm

This famously melodious bird sings from April to June and can even be heard at night: this is extremely rare for passeriformes. In addition, it has a varied and tuneful repertoire. This bird is difficult to see, as it has ginger-brown plumage and is often hidden in bushes or hedgerows. Now a rare summer visitor to Britain, the nightingale is more common in other parts of Europe.

🐦 The nightingale whistles, trills and gurgles: *"tweet-tweet"*, *"tee-rew-tee-rew"* and *"jug-jug-jug"*.

— *plate 22* —

Starling

Sturnus vulgaris

Average size (tail included): 21 cm
Average wingspan: 37 cm

The starling has a short tail and black plumage flecked in white and brown in winter, and black with violet and green hints in summer. It is smaller than the blackbird and, unlike this bird, does not hop along the ground but waddles about nodding its head. It lives in large groups (except during the breeding season), in fields, woods, urban areas or the countryside, or on the shoreline. Starlings sometimes gather together in groups of several hundred thousand, undertaking incredible arabesques and turns in flight, without ever colliding with each other. These flocks form at dusk when the birds come together to roost. The starling eats insects and fruit, using its beak to probe into lawns and seaweed in order to find its food.

🐦 The starling chatters: its song includes gratings, clicking, imitations of other birdsongs and even mobile phone ring tones!

— *plate 23* —

 *Part Two*

OTHER BIRDS

This section deals with the birds that are not classed in the order of passeriformes (the passerines), sometimes simply grouped as "non-passeriformes". There are about thirty orders, each with one or more families within it. You will see here one or more species of bird from 17 different orders. The way birds are classified is always changing as scientists gain more knowledge, so sometimes birds are moved from one order to another or are grouped in a different way. We have indicated some species where scientists are debating their order.

All birds have a syrinx. As a result, the non-passeriformes are not silent, but they are not considered to be good "singers", so we only point out some recognisable songs.

The mallard duck, seen here in his bright mating plumage, quacks.

Great-spotted cuckoo

Clamator glandarius

Average size (tail included): 39 cm
Average wingspan: 62 cm

Like all cuculiformes, this cuckoo has two toes
pointing forwards and two pointing backwards. The
great spotted cuckoo has a long tail, a dark brown
back flecked with white, a light underside and a small
hooked beak. Its crested skullcap is grey (black in
the young). It flaps and hops on the ground, with its
tail raised. This cuckoo visits Southern Europe and
Western Asia in the summer, migrating to Africa in the
winter. Like the common cuckoo (opposite) it lays its
egg in another bird's nests, often a magpie's, leaving
those parents to raise its young. The great spotted
cuckoo young do not push the other chicks out of the
nest and so are raised alongside them.

☛ The great spotted cuckoo coos nervously:
"krikrikri".

— *plate 24* —

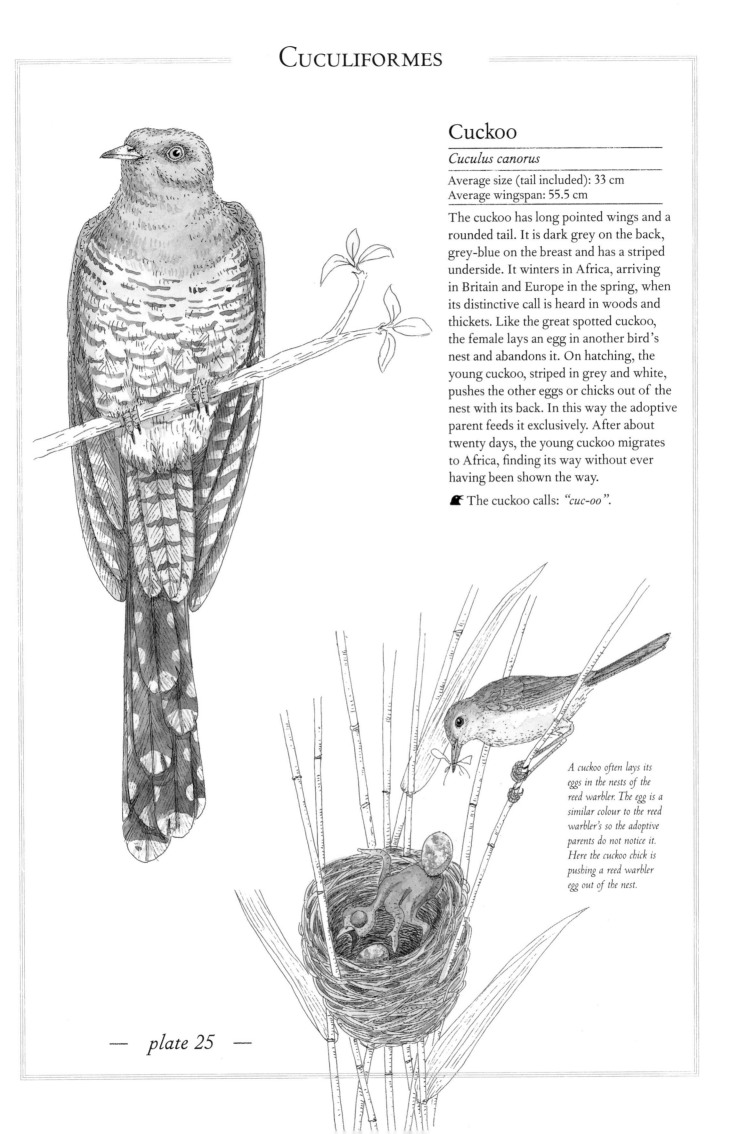

Cuckoo

Cuculus canorus

Average size (tail included): 33 cm
Average wingspan: 55.5 cm

The cuckoo has long pointed wings and a rounded tail. It is dark grey on the back, grey-blue on the breast and has a striped underside. It winters in Africa, arriving in Britain and Europe in the spring, when its distinctive call is heard in woods and thickets. Like the great spotted cuckoo, the female lays an egg in another bird's nest and abandons it. On hatching, the young cuckoo, striped in grey and white, pushes the other eggs or chicks out of the nest with its back. In this way the adoptive parent feeds it exclusively. After about twenty days, the young cuckoo migrates to Africa, finding its way without ever having been shown the way.

🐦 The cuckoo calls: *"cuc-oo"*.

A cuckoo often lays its eggs in the nests of the reed warbler. The egg is a similar colour to the reed warbler's so the adoptive parents do not notice it. Here the cuckoo chick is pushing a reed warbler egg out of the nest.

— *plate 25* —

European roller

Coracias garrulus

Average size (tail included): 31 cm
Average wingspan: 70 cm

The coraciiformes include kingfishers as well as rollers and bee-eaters. This stocky bird is the only roller found in Europe, where it is a summer visitor to southern regions. It has blue and green plumage across the head, part of its wings and the tail; its back is ginger. With its black hooked beak, the European roller mainly catches large insects, such as crickets, but it also eats worms, frogs, lizards and even small birds. It migrates to the far south of Africa in the winter.

🕊 The European roller has a grating and noisy cry: *"rak-ak"*.

fig. 1

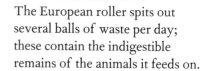

The European roller spits out several balls of waste per day; these contain the indigestible remains of the animals it feeds on.

European bee-eater

Merops apiaster

Average size (tail included): 28 cm
Average wingspan: 47 cm

A summer visitor to Southern Europe and Central Asia, the European bee-eater is an acrobat in the air, but awkward on the ground. It is multi-coloured: its skullcap and back are brown-ginger, it has a yellow neck, a blue-green underside and wings. Its arched beak wears down as it digs out its burrows in banks. It feeds on insects, often bees, as its name would suggest. In autumn, the bee-eater migrates to Africa where food is more plentiful.

🕊 The European bee-eater lets out a series of rolling cries: *"grruup-grruup-grruup"*.

— *plate 26* —

fig. 2

Hoopoe

Upupa epops

Average size (tail included): 27 cm
Average wingspan: 44 cm

The hoopoe's orange plumage is crossed with black on the wings and the tail. It has a crown of orange and black feathers which it raises up when excited. The hoopoe probes for insects with its long, thin beak in mud and other places. A migratory bird, it moves between the European mainland and Africa, but often some birds overshoot and arrive on the south coast of England in spring. Some scientists now classify the hoopoe in a different order than the coraciiformes.

🐦 The hoopoe has a low, loud song to which it owes its name: *"houp-houp-houp"*.

— *plate 27* —

Black woodpecker

Dryocopus martius

Average size (tail included): 46 cm
Average wingspan: 66 cm

The piciformes order includes the woodpecker family. The black woodpecker is the largest in Europe and is quite common, although it is not found in Britain. It is black, but its skullcap is red. Like all woodpeckers, it climbs up tree trunks with its hooked claws and its tail, that it uses as a support. Its beak drumming can be heard from far away. Hunting for insects, it strikes the branches or the trunk with its powerful beak and can hammer 20 blows in less than 3 seconds. In order to withstand the violent shocks, its brain is attached to its skull with shock-absorbing muscles.

🦅 The black woodpecker emits a loud whistling note: *"kree-kree-kree"*.

— *plate 28* —

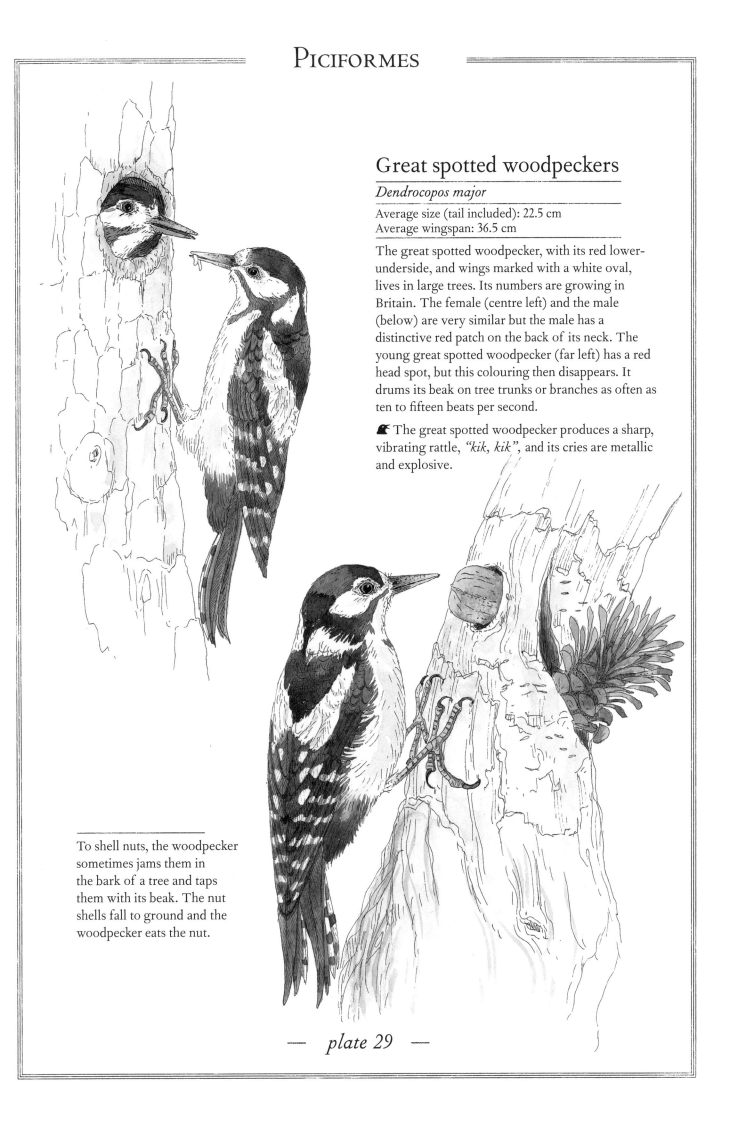

Great spotted woodpeckers

Dendrocopos major

Average size (tail included): 22.5 cm
Average wingspan: 36.5 cm

The great spotted woodpecker, with its red lower-underside, and wings marked with a white oval, lives in large trees. Its numbers are growing in Britain. The female (centre left) and the male (below) are very similar but the male has a distinctive red patch on the back of its neck. The young great spotted woodpecker (far left) has a red head spot, but this colouring then disappears. It drums its beak on tree trunks or branches as often as ten to fifteen beats per second.

🐦 The great spotted woodpecker produces a sharp, vibrating rattle, *"kik, kik"*, and its cries are metallic and explosive.

To shell nuts, the woodpecker sometimes jams them in the bark of a tree and taps them with its beak. The nut shells fall to ground and the woodpecker eats the nut.

— *plate 29* —

Eurasian eagle owl

Bubo bubo

Average size (tail included): 72 cm
Average wingspan: 170 cm

The strigiformes are owls! Found across Europe and Asia but not in Britain, the Eurasian eagle owl is the largest of these nocturnal birds of prey. It has a brown-black back and its face and skullcap are a mottled fawn; its fawn underside has a black vertical wave pattern. It hunts at night using its sharp hearing and its amazing vision. It attacks its prey with its sharp black claws. Its call can be heard up to 5 km away after sunset.

🖝 The Eurasian eagle owl produces a deep resonant call: *"ooh-hu"* .

— *plate 30* —

Barn owl

Tyto alba

Average size (tail included): 36 cm
Average wingspan: 90 cm

The barn owl is rarely seen, but it is relatively common. It has a ginger-grey back, a heart-shaped face and white underside. The disk of feathers on its face collects and focuses sound, which it hears with its two ears on either side of its eyes. These are differently shapes and sited at different levels, enabling it to locate its prey even in the dark. The owl's super-soft feathers allow it to fly almost silently, so as not to alert its prey, shrews and other small mammals on the ground below. This bird of prey hunts actively from dawn to dusk, but only cries out at night: it's an eerie screeching noise! It nests in attics, barns and sheds.

☛ The barn owl screeches: *"sheeeee, sheeeee"*.

— *plate 31* —

Birds in the apodiformes order cannot walk, but are brilliant at flying. Hummingbirds fall into this category. There are 300 species of these extremely tiny birds. They only live in the Americas. The chirpings of the hummingbirds are whistles that are quite unpleasant to the human ear: a mixture of small high-pitched cries and grating notes.

fig. 1

Anna's hummingbird

Calypte anna

Average size (tail included): 11 cm

For its size, the Anna hummingbird is the fastest animal on Earth. The colours of its plumage are sensational: its throat is a deep pink, and its wings and flanks are emerald green.

fig. 2

fig. 3

Vervian hummingbird

Mellisuga minima

Average size (tail included): 6 cm

The vervian hummingbird's nest is the size of half a walnut shell. At 1 cm long, its eggs are among the smallest of any bird.

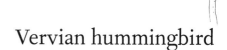

Bee hummingbird,
or Helena hummingbird

Mellisuga helenae

Average size (tail included): 5 cm

At around 5 cm the bee hummingbird is the world's smallest bird!

fig. 4

— *plate 32* —

Swift

Apus apus

Average size (tail included): 16 cm
Average wingspan: 39 cm

The common swift's plumage is dark. Its throat is light. These migratory birds spend nearly all their time in the air. They eat and even mate in flight. They nest in a colony under roof tiles or in hollow trees. They can sleep while flying, as certain parts of their brain remain active, while others are at rest. The swift migrates from Africa to Europe in the summer. It is sometimes confused with the swallow but, as an apodiforme, comes from a completely different order of bird.

The swift lets out a series of piercing cries: *"srriii, srrri, srrii"*.

— plate 33 —

Reeves' pheasant

Syrmaticus reevesii

Average size (tail included): 210 cm
Average wingspan: 80 cm

Originally from China, this pheasant was introduced into Europe
for the sport of hunting. The male Reeves' pheasant has a black
collar and mask, with yellow, black and white plumage. During
the mating season, it waves its tail by raising its rectrices, which
can reach up to 2 m in length. It lives in forests, where it finds
acorns and buds. Critically endangered in China, the
species will perhaps be saved
from extinction by those bred
in Europe.

fig. 1

The galliformes, which include chickens, turkeys and
gamebirds, such as pheasant and partridge, are birds with
a lifestyle based on the ground. They have a solid look
about them, with strong legs and short wings positioned
at a wide angle. There are 300 species in the world.

fig. 2

Northern whitebob

Colinus virginianus

Average size (tail included): 25 cm
Average wingspan: 37.5 cm

The northern whitebob is a small type of quail found
in North America and the Caribbean. Pairs build
their nest on the ground in shallow holes. These
birds live in groups and huddle together when the
weather is cold. When they sense they are in danger,
northern whitebobs scatter in all directions in order
to confuse predators.

— *plate 34* —

fig. 1

Rock ptarmigan

Lagopus muta

Average size (tail included): 35 cm
Average wingspan: 57 cm

The male rock ptarmigan changes its plumage four times a year, the female three times, whereas in general, birds change it twice: in this way they adapt their camouflage to their mountainous or Arctic habitats, as snow comes and goes. In winter the rock ptarmigan is completely white, except for a black spot at the very end of the tail. In summer, its back is crossed with brown and black, and its belly is white. In autumn, its plumage is shorter; it is greyish, flecked in white on the upper side, and always white underneath. In Britain, the ptarmigan is found only in the mountain wildernesses of the Scottish highlands.

🐦 The rock ptarmigan's cry is a dry and grating *"kreurreukreu"*.

fig. 2

Black grouse

Tetrao tetrix

Average size (tail included): 50 cm
Average wingspan: 72 cm

The male black grouse has a black plumage with hints of blue, a red growth, called a "wattle", above its beak, and a white tail in the shape of a lyre (a type of harp). In spring the males gather together in high mountain pastures and bogs to attract a female mate. They compete with each other using their cries and feather displays. The black grouse lives mainly in the forests of Northern Europe, including Scotland.

🐦 The black grouse coos, interspersing its song with hissings: *"tchou-iischt"*.

— *plate 35* —

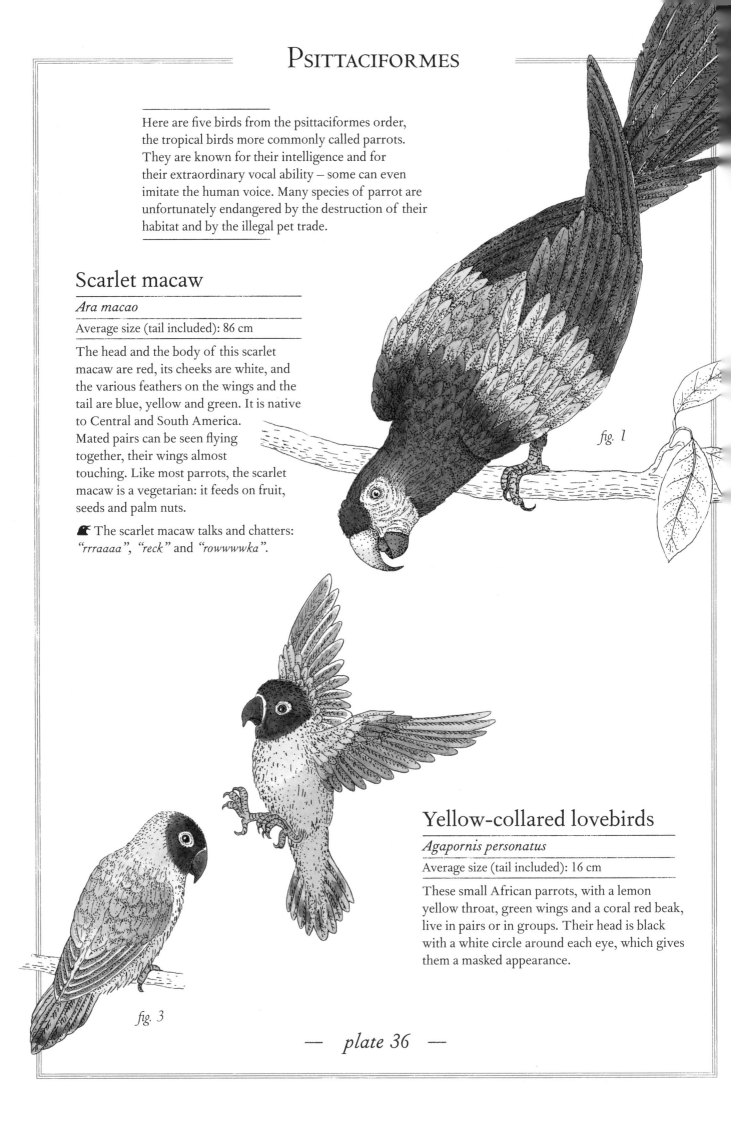

Here are five birds from the psittaciformes order, the tropical birds more commonly called parrots. They are known for their intelligence and for their extraordinary vocal ability – some can even imitate the human voice. Many species of parrot are unfortunately endangered by the destruction of their habitat and by the illegal pet trade.

Scarlet macaw

Ara macao

Average size (tail included): 86 cm

The head and the body of this scarlet macaw are red, its cheeks are white, and the various feathers on the wings and the tail are blue, yellow and green. It is native to Central and South America. Mated pairs can be seen flying together, their wings almost touching. Like most parrots, the scarlet macaw is a vegetarian: it feeds on fruit, seeds and palm nuts.

🐦 The scarlet macaw talks and chatters: *"rrraaaa"*, *"reck"* and *"rowwwwka"*.

fig. 1

fig. 3

Yellow-collared lovebirds

Agapornis personatus

Average size (tail included): 16 cm

These small African parrots, with a lemon yellow throat, green wings and a coral red beak, live in pairs or in groups. Their head is black with a white circle around each eye, which gives them a masked appearance.

— *plate 36* —

fig. 2

Sulphur-crested cockatoo

Cacatua galerita

Average size (tail included): 55 cm

This large, noisy parrot from Australia and other nearby islands is white and its crest is made up of six yellow feathers. It likes to perch in the trees of the mangrove swamps or close to rivers. It flies at very high altitudes. Sulphur-crested cockatoos live in pairs or in small groups. A few cuckatoos perch in trees to act as lookouts while the rest are feeding on the ground; the lookouts raise the alarm in the event of danger.

🐦 The sulphur-crested cockatoo squawks *"ah-yai-yah"* or *"kai-yah"*.

— *plate 37* —

Kakapo

Strigops habroptila

Average size (tail included): 60 cm

This nocturnal parrot with yellow-green plumage lives in New Zealand. The male makes varied and noisy cries to attract the female's attention, calling out for eight hours a night at certain times of year. The kakapo is in fact the noisiest bird on Earth. This species is the only flightless parrot. It is critically endangered because European settlers introduced new predators such as cats and rats which could easily catch these slow-moving ground birds.

🐦 The male kakapo lets out 20 consecutive *"booms"* then one *"tchig"* sound.

— *plate 38* —

Budgerigar

Melopsittacus undulatus

Average size (tail included): 18 cm
Average wingspan: 30 cm

This small, noisy Australian parrot is colourful: its head and its wings are yellow and grey; its body is green with darker wave-markings across its back. It also has black pearl marks around the neck. The small soft swelling found above its beak, called the "cere", is blue in the male. Blue-white-black specimens exist, which are the result of cross-breeding in captivity. The budgerigar is often kept as a pet and some have escaped to live in the wild in Europe.

☛ The budgerigar chatters: its repertoire of cries is varied, and it can be taught to whistle and talk.

— *plate 39* —

Scarlet ibis

Eudocimus ruber

Average size (tail included): 61 cm
Average wingspan: 101 cm

As its name suggests, this ibis' plumage is red. Its grey beak is long, slender and hooked. The scarlet ibis fishes for prawns and crabs in the mangrove swamps of Central and South America. The prawns and crabs have a pigment, carotenoid, which gives the bird its bright colour (young birds have brown feathers). It flies in flocks high in the sky in a V-formation and perches on the treetops. A victim of poaching because of its magnificent feathers, the scarlet ibis is now protected in many countries.

The scarlet ibis lets out a raucous, nasal cry.

— *plate 40* —

African sacred ibis

Threskiornis aethiopicus

Average size (tail included): 89 cm
Average wingspan: 117 cm

The African sacred ibis has a hooked beak, black and white wings, a white underside and a featherless grey neck. This large wader was sacred in Ancient Egypt and a symbol of Thoth, god of wisdom and science. It lives in sub-Saharan Africa, close to humans. It has a varied diet, feeding on the bodies of dead animals, fresh water animals and insects. Sacred ibis that escaped from captivity have settled on the French Atlantic coast and a few other places in Europe.

✆ The African sacred ibis has many calls, *including a "whoot-whoot-whoot-whooeeoh" and a "pyuk-pyuk-peuk-peuk-pek-peuk"* call.

— *plate 41* —

fig. 1

Australian pelican

Pelecanus conspicillatus

Average size (tail included): 188 cm
Average wingspan: 245 cm

This large white pelican, with partly black wings, lives in Australia and other islands of Oceania, close to fresh water. Under its long yellow beak, it has a large pocket of yellow or pink skin, which becomes bright red during the mating season. As in all pelicans, this pocket is used as a fishing net: it plunges its head under the water and opens its beak to catch a fish. When it brings up its head, it presses its beak against its chest to drain away the water, leaving just the fish to eat.

The Australian spectacled pelican yaps, grunts and clacks its beak.

Brown pelican

Pelecanus occidentalis

Average size (tail included): 152 cm
Average wingspan: 216 cm

The brown pelican lives in the Americas. The adult has a yellow head, a white neck and a grey-brown body. Long wide wings allow it to glide over the sea. A water bird, it is clumsy on the ground.

The brown pelican is silent when not in a colony. Its cries are jarring and deep.

fig. 2

— *plate 42* —

fig. 3

Imperial shag

Phalacrocorax atriceps

Average size (tail included): 76 cm

The imperial shag has four toes joined together by pink webbing. Its eyes are ringed in blue, and it has a black crest on its head that disappears during the nesting season. Its back is black, and it has a white belly and underside. This seabird swims on the surface of the water but fishes for its prey by diving. It is found in Antarctica and in Patagonia, at the tip of South America. Scientists now often put shags and gannets in a separate order from the pelecaniformes, called the "suliformes".

fig. 4

Gannet

Morus bassanus

Average size (tail included): 94 cm
Average wingspan: 174 cm

The gannet is a large, majestic seabird. It lives in the North Atlantic, breeding in large colonies on rocky cliffs and islands around northern coasts, particularly those of Britain and Ireland. To fish, it dives into the water at great speed, plunging to depths of over 10 m. This amazing feat is made possible by a reinforced skull and pockets of air on its chest that absorb the shock of impact with the water.

— *plate 43* —

Some scientists limit the order of ciconiiformes to the stork family. Others believe that the order should include more bird families.

White stork

Ciconia ciconia

Average size (tail included): 108 cm
Average wingspan: 205 cm

The white stork lives almost everywhere in Europe, although it is a rare visitor to Britain. It is white, with black flight feathers, a red-orange pointed beak and long legs. At the end of July, storks migrate to Southern Africa to spend the winter there. Unlike some other migratory birds, the young stork has to learn the route from its parents. It makes its first journey with its family but will eventually travel alone. To find their way, migratory birds use the sun (which rises in the east) and landscape features: picking out rivers and hills. They are also sensitive to the Earth's magnetic field.

🕊 The stork is quite a silent bird, and communicates by tapping its beak to make a series of sounds: *"clak-clak-clak"*.

— *plate 44* —

Grey heron

Ardea cinerea

Average size (tail included): 94 cm
Average wingspan: 185 cm

A large grey bird, with a white head, yellow
beak and black crest, the grey heron is
sometimes grouped with the pelecaniformes.
Unlike storks and cranes, it flies with its neck
folded. Found across Europe, including Britain,
it hunts in shallow water, standing motionless,
then uses its dagger-shaped beak to strike
its prey: fish, amphibians, reptiles and small
mammals. After eating, it brings up balls of
undigested fur. The heron nests high up in trees
and lays three or five eggs. Sometimes the last
chick to hatch, weaker than the rest, dies and is
eaten by its brothers and sisters.

🐦 The grey heron lets out cries of *"khreeik"*.

Heron tracks (14 cm long, 12.5 cm
wide) can be seen in the mud with
four clawed toes, including a thumb
at the back.

— *plate 45* —

Greylag goose

Anser anser

Average size (tail included): 84 cm
Average wingspan: 165 cm

This common goose's long neck, back and wings are a grey-brown colour. Its body is a lighter colour, its rump white, and its webbed feet are pink. Greylag geese hold the record for flying at high altitudes, along with cranes and vultures. They have adapted to be able to fly at these heights as they have a special type of red blood cell which carries oxygen to their muscles very efficiently. Their V flying formation can be seen in the sky, when they migrate or move between feeding areas.

Greylag geese honk: *"gah-gah-gah"* or *"onk-onk"*.

— *plate 46* —

FALCONIFORMES

Bald eagle

Haliaeetus leucocephalus

Average size (tail included): 96 cm
Average wingspan: 200 cm

This large brown bird of prey has a white tail and head. Its hooked beak is sharp and its eyes are yellow. It looks for living prey, such as coots, ducks, field mice and even hares, and it fishes on the surface of the water. Its sharp talons are powerful. It only lives in North America and is the emblem of the United States.

🦅 The bald eagle lets out cries of *"kleek-kik-ik-ik-ik"*.

fig. 1

The falconiformes order includes many types of bird of prey. Some scientists have separated these out into more orders, placing the eagles and buzzards, for example, in the order accipitroforme

Golden eagle

Aquila chrysaetos

Average size (tail included): 90 cm
Average wingspan: 190 cm

The golden eagle has eyesight seven times more powerful than that of a human being. As it glides high in the sky, it uses its amazing sight to watch out for prey: mammals such as rabbits and hares. Eagles mate for life and build enormous nests high up in the mountains. The male and female take turns to watch over the eggs. This eagle is found across the Northern Hemisphere but it is very rare in Britain.

🦅 The golden eagle lets out a cry: *"hiey"*.

fig. 2

— *plate 47* —

Common buzzard

Buteo buteo

Average size (tail included): 57 cm
Average wingspan: 120 cm

A very common bird of prey, the buzzard lives in the countryside and forests, often close to villages and houses. It is brown, with white markings on the underside of the wings. Its wings are wide and rounded at the ends and it has a fanned tail. From its perch at the top of a tree, it looks for voles, frogs, worms or insects.

The common buzzard mews: *"kiey"*.

fig. 3

FALCONIFORMES

American kestrel

Falco sparverius

Average size (tail included): 27 cm
Average wingspan: 55 cm

The male American kestrel has a ginger-brown back and tail, a black mark under the eye and a white breast (the female's is darker). It lives on the edge of forests or in cities in North America. This tiny falcon's nest can be found in hollows in trees.

🕊 The American kestrel cries: *"klee-klee-klee"* and *"killy-killy-killy-killy"*.

fig. 1

Andean condor

Vultur gryphus

Average size (tail included): 130 cm
Average wingspan: 300 cm

The Andean condor has metallic black plumage. Unlike the female, the male has a white collar and a crest on its head. The head of this gigantic mountain bird is featherless. Its beak enables it to tear through the flesh of the dead animals on which it feeds. As its name suggests, it lives in the Andes mountains, in South America. Some scientists separate condors into a different order from the falconiformes.

fig. 2

Falconiformes have hooked beaks used for tearing meat from its prey. They are carnivores.

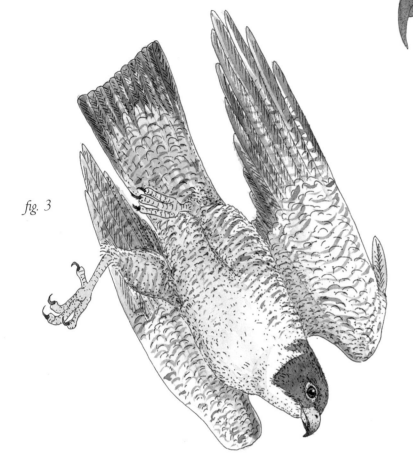

fig. 3

Peregrine falcon

Falco peregrinus

Average size (tail included): 50 cm
Average wingspan: 105 cm

The peregrine falcon has a black head but a pale throat, which makes it look as if it is wearing a helmet. It lives alone in hills and mountains, but also in urban areas and on the coast. It flies at an average speed of 130 to 180 km/h, but can dive at over 200 km/h to catch its prey! It is the fastest bird on Earth. Several pairs of falcons now regularly nest in London.

☛ The peregrine falcon lets out cries of *"kak-kak-kak"*.

The peregrine falcon catches its prey in flight. It helps control the pigeon population in some cities.

— *plate 48* —

Great black-backed gull

Larus marinus

Average size (tail included): 72 cm
Average wingspan: 159 cm

The great black-backed gull is the largest of the gulls. With its white head and body, black wings, light yellow beak, ringed eyes and webbed feet, it can be seen on the coasts of Europe and North America. It builds its nest on the ground or in a hollow in rocks, which it lines with seaweed and grasses.

The great black-backed gull cries out: *"oow-oow-oow"*.

fig. 1

Puffin

Fratercula arctica

Average size (tail included): 27.5 cm
Average wingspan: 55 cm

This bird has a black skullcap and wings, a white body, white rings around the eyes, and a large orange-and-grey beak. Its spends most of its life at sea. In spring, the puffin nests in grassy cliffs, laying its eggs in underground burrows. It brings fish to its chicks in its beak. The puffin's bright colours and clown-like waddle make it a well-loved bird but it is now endangered, its numbers affected by pollution and possibly climate change.

The puffin moans plaintively: *"arrr-ouh"*.

— *plate 49* —

Black-headed gull

Larus ridibundus

Average size (tail included): 40 cm
Average wingspan: 99 cm

Despite its name, this gull has a brown head in spring and summer, a white body, grey wings and orange beak and legs. Most of the year the gull has a white head with a dark patch behind the eye. It lives in places where there is fresh water. Contrary to popular belief, the gull is not a seabird. It breeds inland, alongside streams, lakes, ponds and marshes.

The cry of the black-headed gull is distinctive and raucous: *"kouarrr"*.

— *plate 50* —

Oystercatcher

Haematopus ostralegus

Average size (tail included): 43 cm
Average wingspan: 83 cm

With its black head and back, long, red-orange beak
and legs, the oystercatcher is a distinctive bird to spot
along our coasts. Despite its name, it eats few oysters,
but prefers cockles, crabs and prawns which it finds at
low tide. It uses its beak to hammer open shells or slides
its beak inside shellfish to cut them open. If other birds
get too close to its eggs or its young, it will attack them!

🐦 The oystercatcher has a shrill cry: *"klip-klip-klip"*.

The oystercatcher's nest is a simple dip
in the soil, lined with seaweed and shells.
Its eggs are speckled so that they are hard
to spot on the ground. The oystercatcher
relies on this camouflage to protect its nest
from predators.

— *plate 51* —

Razorbill

Alca torda

Average size (tail included): 38 cm
Average wingspan: 65 cm

The razorbill lives on the rocky coasts of the North Atlantic. This bird has a black head and back all year round, except in winter, when its head is white. It flies fast, close to the surface of the water, using its short, rounded wings. It can swim well underwater, its wings acting as fins.

☛ The razorbill has a harsh cry, and is at its noisiest when it is in a flock.

— *plate 52* —

Sooty tern

Sterna fuscata

Average size (tail included): 33 cm
Average wingspan: 80 cm

The sooty tern is a seabird of the tropical oceans. With its pointed wings and forked tail, it is a lightweight flyer who seldom settles on the ground except during the breeding season. It sleeps in flight and looks for food out at sea on the surface of the water, so it does not need to dive. Its skullcap and its coat are soot black, hence its name. Seabirds often have dark plumage on their upper side, and light underneath. This is an adaptation that enables them to be less easily detected by their prey, the fish.

🖋 The sooty tern has a grating caw.

— *plate 53* —

Common tern

Sterna hirundo

Average size (tail included): 33 cm
Average wingspan: 89 cm

The common tern, a bird with a black skullcap, white plumage and red legs, lives in a noisy flock. Its red beak, which has a black mark, distinguishes it from the Arctic tern. The common tern is found along coasts, rivers and lakes. It feeds on many different species of fish, provided that they are no larger than a few centimetres. It is sometimes called the "swallow of the sea" because of its graceful flight. This migratory bird breeds across the Northern Hemisphere but flies far to the south for the winter months.

The common tern lets out rapid cries: *"kirri-kirri-kirri"* and *"kikikiki"*.

Southern giant petrel

Macronectes giganteus

Average size (tail included): 92 cm
Average wingspan: 200 cm

Like all birds in the procellariiformes category, this imposing seabird has salt glands close to its huge nostrils. These allow it to extract excess salt absorbed from seawater, which it expels through its nose. The southern giant petrel is a scavenger of the southern oceans, eating what meat it can find. It keeps a close eye on penguin colonies, feeding on dead birds and chicks.

Wandering albatross

Diomedea exulans

Average size (tail included): 122.5 cm
Average wingspan: 290 cm

The wandering albatross has the largest wingspan of any bird. It is speckled brown with black tips to its long wings. It catches its prey, such as squid, with its thick 18 cm beak, by floating on the water. A locking mechanism in its wings enables it to fly for several days without tiring, and without setting down. The wandering albatross is generally found in the Southern Hemisphere and breeds on the islands off Antarctica.

🐦 This bird is silent over water but makes guttural, quavering sounds when it fights over food.

— *plate 54* —

Emperor penguins

Aptenodytes forsteri

Average size (tail included): 114 cm

Emperor penguins are the largest penguin. They have a black back, head and webbed feet, with a white body and a yellow mark on the ears. On land, they live standing up on the ice of Antarctica, in colonies of several thousand pairs. They cannot fly. They walk to and from the sea by waddling or sliding on their stomach. They are exceptionally good swimmers and can get down to depths of 400 m in order to catch fish and krill. Their flat and rigid wings act as fins.

🐦 The emperor penguin has a system of complex cries that enables it to recognise other penguins and to locate their chick among thousands of others. This cry is a sort of *"ouiiinnnn, ouin, ouin, ouinnnnn"*.

— *plate 55* —

Ostrich

Struthio camelus

Average size (tail included): 243 cm

The ostrich weighs 100 kg on average, although the male can weigh as much 140 kg. It is the heaviest bird on Earth! This huge bird has a long pink neck and legs. The male has black wing feathers, while the female's are grey-brown. The common ostrich cannot fly because it does not have strong enough wing muscles, but it runs very fast. It can reach speeds of over 70 km/h and jump up to 1.5 m in height and 4 m in length across the African grasslands where it lives.

🐦 The common ostrich lets out resonant cries: *"boo-boo-boo-hoo"*.

The ostrich egg is the heaviest of all eggs. It weighs between 750 g and 1.6 kg, and is 16 cm high and 13 cm wide (a chicken's egg is 4 cm high). The male digs out a nest in the ground for the female to lay her eggs in.

— plate 56 —

Some scientists limit the order of struthioniformes to the ostrich family. Others believe that the order should include many more of the families of large, flightless birds such as the kiwi.

Southern brown kiwi

Apteryx australis

Average size (tail included): 65 cm

The southern brown kiwi, native to New Zealand, cannot fly and its wings have evolved to be simply stumps. Its brown, strong legs are partly covered in scales. Its plumage is a brownish colour. Unusually for birds, the southern brown kiwi has poor eyesight, but a developed sense of smell. It sniffs to find its food, and plunges its long thin beak into the soil.

🕊 The southern brown kiwi has a shrill whistle, which has given it its name: *"ki-wi"*.

— *plate 57* —

Black-crowned cranes

Balearica pavonina

Average size (tail included): 103 cm
Average wingspan: 190 cm

The black-crowned crane has a dark grey body, primary flight feathers and neck. Under its wings its feathers are white; those on its tail are brown. Its face is black and its cheeks are reddish, with a touch of white at the top. It carries a crest of fine, straight, golden-brown feathers on its head, set out in a crown shape, hence its name. It lives in sub-Saharan Africa, close to water and cattle, pecking at the soil to find insects, molluscs and seeds. Before it flies, it runs along the ground to gather speed for take off.

The black-crowned crane makes a trumpeting sound: *"wonk-ka-wonk"*.

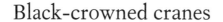

— plate 58 —

Greater flamingo

Phoenicopterus roseus

Average size (tail included): 135 cm
Average wingspan: 150 cm

The phoenicopteriformes are made up of six species of flamingo. These are large aquatic birds, with long legs, a long neck and a special type of beak: the lower jaw is bigger than the upper one. On the edge of each jaw, small strips like a comb filter the water for the crustaceans and algae that the flamingo eats. The greater flamingo is the largest of the flamingos. The colour of its plumage is due to carotenoid pigments, which are found in its favourite prey, the brine shrimp. The greater flamingo is found in Southern Europe, Africa and Southern Asia.

🦅 The greater flamingo lets out a nasal and grating cry: *"kakak"* and *"gagg-agg"*.

— *plate 59* —

GLOSSARY

algae Simple plants that grow in or near water.

altitude The height of an object or a bird in relation to the ground or the sea.

Antarctic The southern area of the Earth near the South Pole.

Arctic The northern area of the Earth near the North Pole.

bird of prey A bird that feeds on the flesh of other animals or birds, using its curved beak and sharp claws or talons.

breed In animals, sexual reproduction to produce young.

camouflage Colour, pattern or shape that allows an object or animal to blend into the background and not be noticed.

cardinal A high-ranking and important clergyman in the Roman Catholic Church.

carnivore An animal that eats mainly meat.

cartilage A type of firm, flexible body tissue.

cephalopod A class of animals, including octopus, squid and cuttlefish, that has tentacles and swims by pushing water out of its body.

class In classification, a large group of living things with similar characteristics.

classification In science, the organisation of different living things into categories, starting with a kingdom (such as animals) then breaking this down into smaller and smaller groups.

compendium A collection of information presented clearly but in few words.

crustacean A large group of animals with soft bodies divided into sections and a hard outer shell. Most live in water, including crabs.

desert An area of land, usually covered with sand, with little or no water.

endangered When a type of plant or animal is described as endangered, it means that it is in danger of dying out and becoming extinct.

extinct When a species dies out completely.

family In classification, a group of living things that are closely related but are not the same species. For instance the albatross family has 21 species, including the wandering albatross.

fledgling A young bird that has just left the nest but is not yet a full-grown adult.

gastropod A large and diverse class of animals. Snails and slugs are gastropods.

habitat The natural home or environment where an animal or a plant usually lives.

insect A class of animals with six legs, a three-sectioned body, no backbone and often wings.

mammal A class of animals that have warm blood, hair or fur. Most give birth to live young and the mothers produce milk to feed them.

mandible A bird's beak is made of two parts – the upper and the lower mandible.

mate The sexual partner of an animal. Used as a verb, it is the sexual act that forms part of animal reproduction.

mating season The time of the year when animals mate.

membrane A thin layer of animal tissue.

migrate When an animal moves from one area or habitat to another, according to the seasons.

migratory The description of an animal that migrates.

mollusc A large group of animals that often has a shell and a muscular foot, including slugs, snails and octopuses.

moult To shed fur or feathers to make way for new ones.

nocturnal An animal that is most active at night and mostly asleep during the day.

offspring Another word for the babies or young of an animal.

order In the classification of living things, an order is a way of grouping similar living things together. An order is a smaller group of living things than a class, and a larger group than a family.

pigment A natural colour occurring in an animal or a plant.

plumage The feathers that cover a bird's body.

poaching The illegal act of hunting or shooting animals.

predator An animal that hunts other animals for food.

prey An animal that is hunted and killed for food by another.

rainforest A thick forest in parts of the world where there is almost daily rainfall.

red blood cell A cell in an animal's blood that carries oxygen to cells around the body.

reptile A class of animals that have a backbone and are usually cold-blooded, with scaly skin.

species A group of animals that can breed together to produce fertile offspring.

syrinx The part of a bird's body that produces noise – similar to the vocal cords of a mammal.

territory Land under the control of a particular country, or animal.

vegetarian An animal that eats mainly vegetables – their fruit, seeds, leaves and stalks.

wingspan The total measurement from tip to tip of a bird's wings when they are outstretched.

INDEX OF PLATES

albatross, wandering ——— 54

bee-eater, European ——— 26

bird of paradise, Raggiana ———
19

blackbird ——— 8

budgerigar ——— 39

bunting, cirl ——— 9

buzzard, common ——— 47

cardinal, northern ——— 19

chaffinch ——— 18

cockatoo, sulphur-crested ———
37

condor, Andean ——— 48

crane, brown crowned ——— 58

cuckoo ——— 25

cuckoo, great spotted ——— 24

eagle, bald ——— 47

eagle, golden ——— 47

fairywren, superb ——— 14

flamingo, greater ——— 59

falcon, peregrine ——— 48

gannet ——— 43

goldcrest ——— 15

goldfinch ——— 5

goose, greylag ——— 46

grouse, black ——— 35

gull, black-headed ——— 50

gull, great black-backed ——— 49

heron, grey ——— 45

hoopoe ——— 27

house martin ——— 11

hummingbird, Anna's ——— 32

hummingbird, bee or Helena
——— 32

hummingbird, Vervain ——— 32

ibis, African sacred ——— 41

ibis, scarlet ——— 40

kakapo ——— 38

kestrel, American ——— 48

kiwi, southern brown ——— 57

lovebird, yellow-collared ———
36

macaw, scarlet ——— 36

magpie ——— 16

nightingale ——— 22

ostrich ——— 56

owl, barn ——— 31

owl, Eurasian eagle ——— 30

oystercatcher ——— 51

pelican, Australian ——— 42

pelican, brown ——— 42

penguin, emperor ——— 55

petrel, southern giant ——— 54

pheasant, Reeves' ——— 34

ptarmigan, rock ——— 35

puffin ——— 49

raven, common ——— 7

razorbill ——— 52

redstart, black ——— 21

robin ——— 3

roller, European ——— 26

shag, imperial ——— 43

sparrow, house ——— 4

starling ——— 23

stonechat, African ——— 17

stonechat, Réunion ——— 17

stork, white ——— 44

sunbird, crimson ——— 20

swallow ——— 12

swift ——— 33

tern, common ——— 53

tern, sooty ——— 53

tit, blue ——— 1

tit, great ——— 2

wagtail, western yellow ——— 6

waxwing, Bohemian ——— 13

whitebob, northern ——— 34

whitethroat, common ——— 10

woodpecker, black ——— 28

woodpecker, great spotted ———
29